W9-ATA-535

The Rise and Fall of Galloping Gertie

written by Bruce Goldstone
illustrated by Tom Leonard

McGraw-Hill
School Division

New York   ·   Farmington

On a windy day in November 1940 the Tacoma Narrows Highway Bridge broke apart and tumbled into the waters of Puget Sound...only four months after it opened. Amazingly, no human lives were lost. Although the bridge stood for only a short time, it made a lasting impact on modern bridge building. It remains one of the landmark disasters of the Twentieth Century.

The sight of the bridge falling was recorded on film and in photographs. Bridge builders, curious amateurs, and science students have viewed these astounding prints and footage ever since. How did people know that the bridge was going to fall? They were warned. The Tacoma Narrows Bridge had been moving since it was first built.

From the day it opened, Tacoma Narrows Bridge was a bridge in motion. The heavy concrete roadway shifted and rolled. Like a wave rippling in a lake, the road floated up and down; a gentle wave rolled from one end of the bridge to the other.

So it was no surprise when at last the bridge began to move too much. But what caused the violent movements that finally tore apart the bridge, and what have bridge builders learned from the rise and fall of the bridge called *Galloping Gertie?*

Bridge builders had made many advances in the first part of the 20th century. They were building longer and longer bridges. They built beautiful and graceful bridges across gaps, rivers, and gorges that were once considered impossible to cross.

In Washington State, about 30 miles south of Seattle, the port city, Tacoma, is located on a body of water called Puget Sound; across the Sound lies the Olympic Peninsula.

For many years, people dreamed of building a bridge across Puget Sound. The peninsula is less than a mile north of Tacoma—without a bridge, the ride from Tacoma to the Olympic Peninsula took more than an hour. Travelers had to drive a giant loop around the Sound. A bridge would make the loop unnecessary, and it would easily cut an hour of travel time off of many trips. Yet the bridge would have to be about 2800 feet long. In 1840, no one had ever built a bridge that long...but by 1940, longer bridges had been successfully built in several cities.

The Tacoma setting presented an irresistible challenge to designers. Eventually, a bridge designer named Leon Moisseiff came up with an exciting scheme for a Tacoma bridge.

Moisseiff's plan called for the type of bridge that had revolutionized bridge-building. He would build a suspension bridge.

A suspension bridge supports the weight of the bridge from above. The roadway hangs from giant cables like clothes from a clothesline, and the cables are attached to firmly planted piers. This powerful bridge design has been used in the construction of all major bridges since the Brooklyn Bridge.

The Brooklyn Bridge, completed in 1883, was the first modern suspension bridge, but the principle on which it is based had been around for a long time. Ancient rope bridges were built in South America, where heavy ropes were hung across a large gorge. More ropes were then hung, or suspended, from the heavy rope cables. The weight of the roadway, and the people who traveled on it, were supported by the cables.

Rope suspension bridges can only hold very limited weights, and it wasn't until the invention of steel cables that suspension bridges became practical for modern use. Today's heavy steel cables can support the enormous weight of concrete roadways, cars, trucks, and other traffic.

Before the 1880s, people did not think that suspension bridges would work. They doubted that the cables would be strong enough. The success of the Brooklyn Bridge in New York changed that, though, and convinced people that suspension bridges were the bridges of the future.

Bridge designers began to build longer and longer suspension bridges. In 1931, the George Washington Bridge, connecting Manhattan and New Jersey, was opened. At 3500 feet long, it was more than twice as long as the Brooklyn Bridge. Six years later, the Golden Gate Bridge in San Francisco became the longest suspension bridge in the world.

As designers got better and better at creating suspension bridges, they tried for new goals. They tried to create lighter bridges by using fewer supports or different roadway materials. Lighter bridges were easier to support and less expensive to build.

Builders also created bridges that were narrower and narrower. They did not yet think that the narrowness of a bridge was related to its sturdiness. The ratio, or relation, between a bridge's length and width began to increase. The Brooklyn Bridge was 19 times longer than it was wide, and the George Washington Bridge was 33 times longer than its width—but Moisseiff's plan for the Tacoma Narrows Bridge was even more extreme.

5

Leon Moisseiff planned to build a bridge that was 72 times longer than it was wide; he developed this plan based on studies of the traffic in the Tacoma area.

Experts studied traffic patterns in the area carefully and decided that any bridge over Puget Sound was in an unusual situation.

Most suspension bridges, like the Brooklyn Bridge and the Golden Gate Bridge, were four lanes wide, with two lanes of traffic traveling in each direction. Since the traffic patterns near Tacoma were not as busy, the builders decided that the bridge only needed two lanes, one in each direction.

Only after the bridge was built did people realize what an important, and unfortunate, decision this was.

Some Major Suspension Bridges Before 1940

Bridge	Year Completed	Length (feet)	Width (feet)	Ratio of Width to Length
Brooklyn	1883	1595	85	1 to 19
Williamsburg	1903	1600	114	1 to 14
George Washington	1931	3500	106	1 to 33
Golden Gate	1937	4200	89	1 to 47
Bronx–Whitestone	1939	2300	74	1 to 31
Tacoma Narrows	1940	2800	39	1 to 72

Moisseiff and the other designers who created the Tacoma Bridge were very careful. After planning the bridge on paper, they used many tests to make sure the bridge would be safe.

One of the experts who helped design the bridge was Professor F. B. Farquharson, who was a wind expert at the University of Washington. His job was to think about how wind would affect the bridge. To see how the design would stand up to strong winds, he used a new testing tool called a *wind tunnel*, which helped designers check the bridge's strength against wind.

Farquharson placed a model of the bridge in the wind tunnel. The Tacoma model passed the wind tunnel test, which convinced people that the design would stand up to strong winds.

Unfortunately, the wind tunnel was a new invention in the 1930s, when the bridge was being tested. While the results of the test were accurate, they were also very limited. It was true that the Tacoma Bridge could withstand the forces of very strong wind storms, but the wind tunnel did not test for the normal wind conditions over Puget Sound.

Convinced that the design was strong and safe, builders went to work on the Tacoma Narrows Bridge. The long two-lane bridge was much lighter than a four-lane bridge like the George Washington Bridge.

By the time the road was completed, the designers knew that there was something unusual about the bridge—it moved. Actually, all suspension bridges move a little bit; the movement helps them to adapt to changing wind conditions. The Tacoma bridge was unusual simply because it moved so much.

The designers were concerned, but did not panic; they were convinced that the bridge was safe, and allowed it to open on July 1st, 1940.

People were curious about the moving bridge. Driving across the bridge was like riding a roller coaster. Sometimes drivers would lose sight of the car in front of them as it dipped into the bottom of a wave.

You might think that people would be frightened of a moving bridge, and you might think that they would avoid it, afraid that it might fall down. Perhaps some people did stay away, but even more came to ride the roller-coaster bridge!

The bridge attracted far more people than predicted. Soon they gave the bridge an affectionate nickname: *Galloping Gertie*. People came from far and near to ride on the bouncy bridge and Gertie was a big success.

The bridge designers did take some steps to steady Gertie's rolling. They added a new metal support to stiffen the bridge a little but these supports did not have much effect. Everyone was still convinced that the bridge design was unusual, but not risky.

Then on November 7th, 1940, the fun clearly turned to danger. It was a windy day, but the winds were not at the level of a hurricane. They were blowing about 43 miles per hour.

However, observers noticed that these winds were having a strong effect on Galloping Gertie. The bridge's gentle rolling turned violent and it began to twist back and forth.

Luckily, people recognized that the bridge was too dangerous to cross, and it was closed to traffic.

Clark Eldridge, one of the bridge's designers, was called by a friend and warned about the sudden changes in Gertie's movements. Eldridge went to the bridge to observe it firsthand.

Later, Eldridge wrote a first-hand description of the disaster. When he arrived, the twisting movements had already begun. The bridge was "swaying wildly," and it was "possible first to see the entire bottom side" of the roadway and then the top.

One reporter had driven across to get an exciting eyewitness view, but he had to leave his car behind and run for safety. The car remained on the bridge as it twisted up and down.

Hundreds of people came to watch Gertie's wild shifting; Professor Farquharson, the wind expert, recorded the entire event with a movie camera.

After some time, Eldridge noted that "the main span was still rolling badly and the east side span was still quiet...At that time it appeared that should the wind die down, the span would perhaps come to a rest." Then the wind did begin to lessen....

Unfortunately, it was too late—the bridge had already twisted too far. At 11:10 in the morning, observers looked on with dismay as one steel section fell into the waters of Puget Sound. Once the first section fell, the rest happened very quickly. Section after section dropped into the water. The single car plunged into the water and Galloping Gertie fell apart in front of hundreds of observers.

It was one of the most recorded disasters of all time. Professor Farquharson's film captured the twisting and falling of the bridge, and many other people had photographs of the event. They show a complete record of the remarkable and horrifying sight.

Fortunately no human lives were lost when Gertie fell apart, but why had Galloping Gertie failed? What forces pulled apart the Tacoma Narrows Bridge? Was it a mean trick by some unknown immortals? What else could it be? It was time to search out the clues that would provide answers.

Suspension Bridges

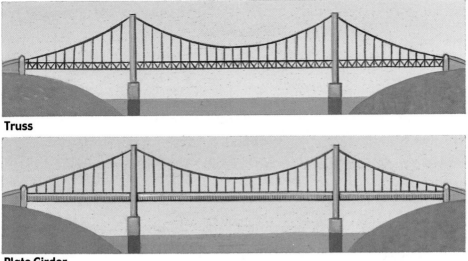

Truss

Plate Girder

At first the problem seemed murky and confusing, but eventually experts realized that many problems, not just one, had led to the disaster.

The fact that the bridge was so long and narrow was one key cause—a wider bridge would not have moved as much in the same conditions. The decision to build a two-lane bridge made sense based on the traffic survey, but it turned out to have been an unsafe choice.

The bridge design itself was another problem. Most suspension bridges are supported by heavy trusses—these iron supports keep the bridge from shifting down under the weight of cars. Instead of trusses, the builders of the Tacoma Narrows bridge used eight-foot metal strips called *plate girders*, which had been successfully used in shorter, wider bridges. It was not until the Galloping Gertie disaster that designers realized they were not suitable for longer bridges.

Another important cause of the bridge disaster was the wind—the wind tunnel testing had not been sufficient. If experts had known how strongly the bridge responded to light winds, the normal wind conditions in the area, they may have been able to correct the problem.

Leon Moisseiff always accepted the blame for the disaster, yet a lot of the problems really occurred because science galloped ahead of safety. Designers simply didn't know enough about wind testing and wind science.

After the disaster, bridge builders took a hard look at the bridges that were currently standing, and made many improvements to ensure that similar disasters didn't happen in other parts of the country. They added trusses to certain bridges that used the plate girder design, like the Bronx-Whitestone Bridge. Additionally, three and a half million dollars were spent to make safety changes to the Golden Gate Bridge.

Wind tunnel testing also became much more accurate at predicting real-life results; scientists now test every part of a design before a bridge is built.

Scientists have applied their new knowledge to build longer and stronger bridges—the current record-holder is the Akashi Kaikyo in Japan. Engineers were so successful in designing this bridge that it even stood up to a powerful earthquake in 1998.

Perhaps the most fitting monument to the Galloping Gertie tale is found sitting atop the Puget Sound today, where a new Tacoma Narrows Bridge carries travelers quickly and safely from Tacoma to the Olympic Peninsula.

Construction of the new bridge began in 1949, and designers were careful to avoid the problems of the first bridge. They created a bridge that is wider than the original, and carries four lanes of traffic—two in each direction. Unlike Gertie, the new bridge also includes deep trusses. Designers also added a special opening, or gap, down the middle of the bridge, which helps wind flow through the bridge without causing it to move.

Riding across today's Tacoma Narrows Bridge might not be as exciting as a roll across Galloping Gertie, but it is a safe and steady ride. Gertie's rapid rise and fall led to important changes that helped create strong, trustworthy bridges throughout the world.